Blessed With Sails

V. R. Walker

Edited by
Dinah H. Walker

Bloomington, IN  Milton Keynes, UK

authorHOUSE™

AuthorHouse™
1663 Liberty Drive, Suite 200
Bloomington, IN 47403
www.authorhouse.com
Phone: 1-800-839-8640

AuthorHouse™ UK Ltd.
500 Avebury Boulevard
Central Milton Keynes, MK9 2BE
www.authorhouse.co.uk
Phone: 08001974150

First published by AuthorHouse 9/1/2006

ISBN: 1-4259-4116-8 (sc)

Printed in the United States of America
Bloomington, Indiana

This book is printed on acid-free paper.

Dedicated to:

Dinah,
Who has always blessed me with sails.

Contents

Blessed with Sails

Blessed with Sails

When I've traveled with no destination
your sojourn as an apparition
planes my dreams with partitions
into neonatal constellations.

Myths and legends recorded in cuneiform
stirred Sumerians and Minoans
to set sail for celestial moorings
before a red dawn gave sailor's warning.

The Gods cursed man as a semi-creature
but blessed with sails from a bride's nature.

An Ancient Symbol

On the Serengetti plain
by the primal Olduvai gorge
Homo habilis' eyes strain
to gleam embers in the tender.

He blows to increase the heat
and builds the fuel slowly
until the flames are discrete
and aligns the fate of man.

Your primordial fires rekindle
and becomes an ancient symbol.

Blue Jeans

From the first crowded night
that I fumbled with love beads
in the scent of jasmine incense
I have pursued blue jeans.
Even today I float the streets
for another skin worn pair
with fade crested waves
that roll on a sand bar.
But I could never imagine you
even in Calvin Klein.

Candles Are for Lovers

The flame flickers and flirts
like the Hellenic etchings
framed in the cavern of your hair.
It then stands tall, slender and bright
like the bride before floating away
on a midnight song.

Collaboration

When I wake at 2 in the morning
and lie on sheets wet with sweat
I listen to the percussion
as my heart constructs a concert.

If there was only one instrument
performing in my imagination
there would be no notes for the duet
that sings endless musical rounds.

When I am in your company
we create a new symphony.

Creation

Whenever you begin to ebb,
your high tide delivery
leaves little evolving creatures
in my cerebral tidal pool.

Trapped for only a date
with each saline menustrate,
they ravage and scavenge
until my muse is a frenzy.

Dinah of the Sinai

Hear the words of the Rabbi:
"Come and grow old with me
for the best is yet to be";
but he left it up to me
for the delivery.

Dinah's Instruments

The trumpet when you phone;
the trombone when you yawn;
the violin when you sigh;
the clarinet when you stroll;
the flute when you laugh;
the saxophone when you seduce;
the bass when you write;
the drum when you shower;
the piano when you think;
makes the orchestra of my days.

Divine Wind

As I slept, I dreamed I slept
with you while October's frost
stenciled nature's fantasies
on panes watching you and me.

As I dreamed, I watched me dreaming
of caricatures careening
through quick change identities
that sounded like you and me.

Dreams glide on a divine wind
that passion can not suspend.

Entropy

The lighthouse pulverizing storm
wakes the earth, the sky and the sea
and makes a cappuccino shore.

Mixing enthalpy and entropy
the squall breaks porcelain species
and howls with the birth of entities.

Evenings with you roll in waves
that exhausts and becalms me.

The Ice Lady

The shower dresses her
in a clear sequin form.
The water molds her
curves, angles and points
until she melts in my arms.

Just One More Throw

Shops are for making, baking,
mixing and fixing anything
for anyone who crosses thresholds
and carries back artifacts.

In a well swept shop stands
a dusty, spidery potter's wheel.
Its molded clay is brittle
and to far from the center.

I can't break my silence's chasm
when I hear the breath in your voice.
I can't anchor my hand's spasm
when I swam dive into your eyes.

A Mangrove Estuary

In the mangrove estuary
to survive is to vary
the healing of abrasions
with the changing seasons.

Being neither land nor water
and water neither salt nor fresh
embryos swim with nude bathers
whose trysts are the only stress.

In between friendship and our love
we simmer on a solar stove.

Missed Steps

Sit in the sand and talk with me.
Tell me the thoughts that travel
the deepest crevices of your mind
and the feelings that hide
in the remote niches of your heart.
Take the most dangerous step
of your life and let us explore
the frontiers of you.

Morning

The clothes lie like bracket
on the dull oak floor.
I inventory my rhymes
for inspirational reciting
before I check the color
of her eyes.

My Destiny

When shadows consume the room
dimensions dissolve to dust
and I receive a reprieve
for a nocturnal liberty.

When must do, need to and should have
stumble into a black hole
I'm met by my spirit guide
who leads me to you inside.

Sleep may be a necessity
but dreams are my destiny.

My Rainbow

When Newton transfigured the world
he waved a crystal clear prism
before the light of our ancient sun
and created man's first rainbow.

White is all colors and black is none
and the color I see is the one
that is reflected to my retina
and all others are absorbed.

All I can see is what you are not.
All I can not see is what I want.

My Safe Anchor

When night closes my room to the world
and my day becomes a convenient cliché
the wall will reflect the sounds
of your whispers lingering in my ear.

If dreams are the ships we sail into the night
then your breath is the wind filling my sails
and like Ulysses I will return to my home port
and rejoice that I am your only suitor.

Titles, wealth and fame will never compare
to my faithful compass and my safe anchor.

Raynauld's Child

In frozen methane space variety
is a cosmic display of fate's portents
as the sun's brilliant gravity
creates firmament's ornament.

The frozen seas of Jupiter's moon
show tides of sub-glacial forces
as strong as its sister's monsoons
heated from a molten metallic core.

The metaphysics of Halley's and Europa's
are forged and tempered beneath ice flows.

Rebirth

Autumn leaves have shrouded the ground
waiting for winter's bitter bridal gown
but the groom's absence has been denounced
and even the evergreens have turned brown.

Spring grows pristine and immaculate
without irrigation and nitrates
and blossoms consummate to populate
a world that no longer deteriorates.

In an exhausted forest you restored grace
but you remained perennial yet chaste.

The Sea Was as Smooth as Glass

Planning a Caribbean ascent
to an unknown glacial altitude
fears and baggage were left behind.

Working on your Absolut perfect tan
I marveled at how your shadows changed
over your smooth operational terrain.

On a clothing optional beach
I still didn't know your true color.

A Simple Meal

Last night was a brazier
of slow roasting emotions
with a warm pink center.

Quickly seared to seal
in the thick rich juices,
it was a satisfying meal.

A loaf of bread, a jug of mine and thou
were consumed without a sound.

Singing

Mom will sing her hymns a little louder
and pretend everything is all right.
Dad will chuckle a little prouder
and try to keep it out of sight.
I'll sit down to eat some clam chowder
and remember your eyes of delight.

Together and Apart

In the night there is a conclave
when dreams breathe and begin to crave
another harmonic alpha wave.

A gleam from a thinking machine
transmits impressions of a scene
with you as my nocturnal queen.

When reason, time and day depart
we wake together and apart.

Too Many Goals

Even the best of history's actors
could not perform all of your roles
and what you believe to be factors
are nothing more than too many goals.

His desires and requests for sharing
may seem contrived and demanded
but don't contrast us by comparing
for what I have is more than he wanted.

Knowing you has become my requiem
for each moment is a gift in a dream.

Two

Two walking
arm in arm.
Strangers or lovers
or both?
A sleeping, draping embrace.

With Each Breach

The sea spray chases the breeze
filling the dunes with fluids
and sounds echoed in the deep.

Each reaching wave breathes deeper
and rises higher with the tide
that flushes, rinses and unites.

When you are serene into the beach
you change with each time I breach.

Rorschach's Shield

Rorschach's Shield

Like Perseus' it's made of art and craft
but its primary purpose is defense
against evolving realities.

With the precision of Egyptian math
it mirrors images of the sixth sense
and ego's terse set frailties.

Thirdly, its refrains of an epitaph
punctuated in carnal nonsense
will employ tutors of antiquity.

So do not label me as esoteric
for my rise will not be meteoric.

All the Answers

Were we star crossed to join the search
or merely rebellious youth?
The reincarnation of the Lost Generation
trying to revitalize and legitimize
by standing and demanding
the recognition of a glance
or by disturbing a heavenly trance?

Boil, Toil and Trouble

It was a brain's blood boiling summer
just south of the Georgia line.
I was working the Mexican towline
while my buddy drove the Georgia buggy
through moccasin soup.
We'd drink a gallon a day
and watch it roll down our backs
where mosquitoes would slide pass
the drowning chiggers.

The Bridge

East opens the game with innuendo
having learned the lesson of being bold;
South replies with the fullness of life
but is bound with doubt and strife;
When East's repeated bid is dubious
the West's reflexes sound furious;
All marvel at the player who's calm
while North plots for the Grand Slam.
Would cuts or blows be less kind
in this sensuous dance of violence?

Café du Jour

The stage is no larger
than the shade of a small
Platanus orientalis.
As I gaze on the facial clichés
my lyrics scatter their chatter.
The guitar sparkles
like a glass bead screen
for them to project
their ego's allegories.

The Corn Crib

Down in the corn crib
where the foals eat without bibs
a rat snake hides within a crate
among the bones of a field mouse
and it's decimated mate.

Eggs must be gathered
from its mother's feathers
and that runt piglet
must roast on the spit
for the family's Sunday luncheon.

A Country Road

I breast stroke thru the life
that pools around a country road.

My senses ripen in the pine straw bed
and suckle on the musky wet warmth.

My spirit's seed couples with the scene
to gestate until it can be named.

Once you have been down a country road
no other road will seem the same.

The Dance

Campfires guarded in remote caves
carve surrealistic shadows
of couples in syncopated time
as each generation bonds and grows.

Neolithic fertility rhythms
for a rotisserie dance
beat for bistro dates with latte tastes
and nocturnal nonchalance.

We believe mysteries have been solved
but the dance continues to evolve.

Distillation

When he was young he would climb
to garner tribute and fame
and he hoped it would trespass
his own eternal crevasse.

When he had sons he had hoped
that they would have developed
as climbers, not residents
with metered lives in tenements.

In a climber's copper tea kettle
time's flames distill myths to truths.

Dusk Silhouettes

With cemented hands he holds his spear
at the end of a weather shorn pier
and he targets an alligator gar
silhouetted against a sand bar.

Dylan

For bourbon words at tea
I thank the minstrel's creed
"never more, never more".
Ladies' allusion of misdeeds
and whore's betrothal repeated
"never more, never more".
My friend, for gelding me
I curse your youthful end
"forever more, forever more".

The Fiddler Crab

Periscope sights above the sand
target the next hole.
He ejects, scouts and skitters
towards his sanctuary.
The wave peaks and covers
its hypnotic, biogenic hollow
and collapses climatically
to drive him home burdened
with his swollen pride.

Freefall

We maintain Amorphous' floats
to buoy us when we fall
from plastic pedestals.

If you are not afraid to fall,
you may find it isn't so dark or far
or the pedestal so good a home.

Our psychic depths appear darker
and farther when we sense our fear.

Her Dawn

In a carotene colored forest
a crippled doe beds down
and prays for healing before
she smells man scent again.

Summer feasts faded too soon
when sweet acorns promised
the end to her hunger
after a Stonehenge solstice.

Unkept promises predict her sunsets
but she will control the dawn.

Her Mystique

Searching for man's better nature
she knows all of his misery
and bears the scars of departures
on her skin like a diary.

She lives in darkness and smoke
but she sees with crystal clarity
that our lives are merely a pen stroke
written with certain brevity.

If I survive her critique,
I'll visit again her mystique.

Him Lines

Strolling was hard in '68
when bikinis torched the beach
and chased sinew tunes
with their short dated skin.

But it's harder in '86
when I've kept more than lost
because lowered hems measure
the depth of character.

"I Owe a Cock"

There are a variety of poisons
for all the known little treasons.

Some come from the Egyptians
who treat lady mathematicians
with a stony overdose
of well dispersed throws.

Some are offered in a sponge
to encourage the final plunge
of teachers who don't conform
and don't drink water lukewarm.

Some are quick without warning
to reduce to long a mourning
for the lost philosopher
who was to right to defer.

Just Have Faith

What I always deemed permanent
could shadow the scion sun
and the only nature that defeats
the mountain is the nurturing rain.

The infinite hype of a promise
that always points to the cornice
of a grand expansive mansion
sinks below what could have been.

The days are sheets of glacial ice
vanishing in an unknown ocean.

Leaves Are Funny

Leaves are such funny things.

They gather as terraces
in the corner by the pool,
then meander to the other side
and slander their former home.

Leaves are such funny people.

Mangoe's

Among the pastels and the palms
they hear the congoes and the gourds
and the syncopated chords.

Single or couple or group
they dance through their age and time
until body boundaries decline.

They dance to prepare for the dawn.
They dance for tomorrow's test.
They dance for togetherness.

A Mariner's Mother

Her breathing rolls in waves
underneath navy sheets.

Her raspy sounds rush
to me in a cacophony.

Her mineral scents measure
from eons to fertile life.

When dawn wades from within her
I taste her salt on me.

I knew when I was weaned
our bonding would be sprayed
on land, in air and on the sea.

A Midnight Wade

Seeing Shelley's spray
in navy corduroy waves
reminded me to return
to sand and the unborn.

There's still a message to bring
of the siren's missing string
and the succulent treat
that escaped starfish feet.

My Cyrano Days

Our futures formed in the second and third
are nurtured to mature into legend;
then cremated in the fourth element
and decorated across the firmament.

My Cyrano days are rehearsed and recorded
in terse lines that fill my entrails.

No Stones Cast

Laying in fresh mown sweet grass
the earth spins beneath my senses
circumventing the denizens
coined in beaten tarnished bronze.

A Sunday afternoon repose
harvested in ploughman's hands
is the beatified's reward
for a life tried and expired.

Years of service was my penance
before the jester's martyr sentence.

Only the Shadows

Why can't I
see the sunshine
thru the trees?
To watch it
filter thru the trees
and gently flow down
all around me.
Why must I
always be bent forward
looking only at the shadows?

The Price

Memories must be urned
with all that we cremate
when we sell ourselves
to the highest bidder.
And though Maslow's laws
have been satisfied
I bitch about the price.

The Runner

My head feels like a Navajo drum
during the cactus ritual;
beating in rhythm to the squish
of blood soaked socks.
With the morning star
the primeval battle begins,
but this time I can see
the cattails.
Those glorious cattails!

Saline and Silicone

The womb of life
calls people back
like some great marsupial.
They try to regain their heritage
by loitering on some wormwood
resting on a few pillars of salt.
There they remain
until they become like that old man
who sits gazing towards the horizon
with squinting albatross eyes.
Saline and silicone
crystallizing in my eyes
turning them into two rocks off salt.
Saline and silicone
absorbing the moisture from my skin
until I look like some rotten peach
floating on the sea.

Singularity

Meant to be a monument
this mausoleum has caused
charities to gnash their teeth.
So I will pause as I saunter
through the values of antiquity.
I will peer and stare into the cavern
as a late visitor to a tavern
to find that the greater the emptiness
then the greater the singularity.

The Solitary Owl

The solitary owl
anchored in splendored gore
guided his lofty challenge
by the grace of a soft talon.

Through the crews of fossil ooze
and the din that exalts
musicians as the new prophets,
continents move down the tube.

Smiles guarantee the politician's
denial of our merited demise
while the prophets disguise
bile and the crypt's goodbyes.

Then the midnight carousel
of crystalline days and mushroom nights
returns me to the asphalt sea
with ebony dreams of effervescent days.

Stuck in the Middle

Endings do not concern me,
they have their own time.
Beginnings do not concern me,
they have their own energy.

It isn't my great fears
that cause me the most harm;
it is the little fears
that ooze from the periphery.

Disjointed promises from an albatross
are like tails on a double headed toss.

To Know the Place

When it is fulfilled
boulevards are broad
and travel's a thrill
with the route not marred.

When unrequited
a promise is fraud
and trail signs denied
leads me only backwards.

When shared but sworn chaste
there is no forward
but we know the place
and it's our reward.

The Tulip

What would you do to a tulip
in your rhubarb patch?
Pluck it for a Sunday sermon?
Preserve it for determined devouts
who will return home and
watch whispers waste away?

Winning?

I have traveled far to reach this glen
and ask without doubt this question
about why with each critical session
there is no consummate answer.

Time and age and place are gone
with every temporal congestion
whose urgencies are séances
with no reference to compare.

We know how to create and delete
and win without being consecrate.

The Migrant

The Migrant

Your laughter butterflied the aging trees
pollinating our personalities
and your words drooled like ripened fruit
during my feast as your new recruit.

Frosting breezes edged changing seasons
forecasting nature's perennial treasons
so I harvested those brisk autumn times
and stored them in cellars for my rhymes.

The days are not picked by the migrant
who has become the chaff vagrant.

All Night Lovers

On a seven foot sofa
a vintage French cabernet
gives comfortable solace
and morning's forever delayed.

An inebriated daydream
fills the evening with wit
and her breath with fragrant steam
that wets my lust thru the night.

We are always nightlong lovers
when I'm alone and not sober.

Aqualung in '81

The park bench remains encrusted
with mottled paling paint
as my gaited return kneads
memories with mortality.
Over the dew mourning tunes
in Simon's time chimes the toll
for my Madonna.
Then the pretty truths run by
to show their worth to a man's
sex appeal of ninety thou' a year.
The chants of worn plastic
skirting Hamilton reality
charms me until Longime's crime
crows for the third wistful time.

Are Walls Good?

When Atlantis arose from the oceans
citizens hid its secrets of success
to transform machinery into motion
within walls of concentric circles.

When the sea reclaimed the temple
and ritual altar of energy
its secret was forever kept and
passed into ledgend as a mystery.

When my walls at last have fallen down
will you be happy with what you have found?

The Aria

My life is conveniently measured
by the TV guide once a week,
by the bank statement once a month,
by the doctor exam once a year.

You never believed I could sing
but your words are the aria
in this historical opera
performed in an empty theater.

The stage, the story and the score
were written with your entrance and exit.

A Bloated Fish

My mind floats like a bloated fish
ferried on currents of verse
to shores of forgetfulness.

Scales of justice flakes from my ribs
and my words crash to the crabs
as my judges crumble to bribes.

Purgatory should be shared
when both of us spoke and erred.

Café de Mer

When I sit down to the morning fast
and steam my sinuses in coffee
I remember your eyes like tannin pools.

By noon I've returned from last night's cask
to drown in apricots at our café
and the dream of sweet saliva is cruel.

As the sun sets down streets of masts
the warm brie served with brandy
embalms the air in our daily duel.

Every experience is a possessed session.
Does that answer your parting question?

Cardiomyopathy

The morning gnaws
thru nylon drawn incisors
the carrion of last night's debauch.

My brain racing with dopamine
I peel the wet sheets from my back
like a newly shredded skin.

Too many dreams have been strewn
for too many landscape lovers.

The Chameleon

Lines drawn in the grass by shades of color
and lines of traffic stacked by careers
measured our passing with jaded breath
and all I could wish was that I could change.

But in the dimly lit den of cars
and the chorus of deftly felt leaves
age crept over me like the Portuguese
and all I could wish was that I could change.

Claret Residues

An empty swan etched glass
dulled with claret residues
is resting on the minister's pew.

For the old portrait artist
the strokes are no longer deft
and there's no one to play with.

An evening invitation
between designing friends
ended with both offended.

The Diet

Love can consume one and friendship feeds on
    two
but there are too many famines between me
    and you.
There are all the men of your past standing
    before me
and innuendos of anorexiants baiting you.
Will you remember with your slowly starving
    diet
tasting a young man's heart and old man's loins
    for desert?

Dumbo's Ballet

Nightshade flowers
who dance on the hour
decorate my end of the bar.
Tantalizing tarantulas allude
to enticing promises
but I will chase celluloid cuties
in well worn pages.

The Elbo Room

At least I caught your eye
before you lowered them
to your champagne cocktail.
Moves without looks or
looks without moves,
which would have stirred you
to flag in this infectious heat?
Will you and your impromptu date
read this question in the sand?

Etchings

On cold days I would stroll
as though with purpose and pause
in caverns of modern art
like an old connoisseur.

As I gazed at Monet's work
the colors spin until they spill
onto a vacant pastel wall
and form a mural to your allure.

Your visits are masterpieces
leaving only stark charcoal etchings.

Hard to Hear

The quartet plays its chamber music
and when the movement is at its peak
they hold the note in air like a breath.

Long then short and high then low
the bows caress the strings in sharps
and flats whose harmony is designed.

Sometimes listening is hard to hear
when the music resonates between us.

His Grasp

Before I offered you that vintage claret
I knew who'd hold the other glass
and how well she was in your grasp.
Like the Cana wedding there is no deceit
only Socrates' muse's receipt
of words, images and Browning's reach.

Insomnia

Your name brushes my cheek
as I rise from my desire
to find that you aren't there.

The pumping furnace in my chest
ignites the search for your form
but cradles only emptiness.

My heart lays bloody fodder
on the unctuous fields of denial.

Jetties

Why is it when I walk the beach
after a Labor Day festive spree
that I see chipped souvenirs
who stroll but don't seem to breathe?

It is then that your sojourn
with ramrod back just sunburned
and peaceful sleep unearned
jetties me in coke and bourbon.

The Physics of the Night

Mineral residues of wasted tears
scents too many unknown motel pillows
because waking single to a morning
is a gyroscope to time's terrain.

Socrates' theory of causality
echoes in the court's elicit verdict
and the ecumenical canons
is an absence of evidence.

How can the universe be sane
when light is mass, energy and time?

Rhyme Infarct

Sitting in half lit rooms
I work thru tinted windows
mirroring afternoons
as my mourning sin slows.

Garlic chicken fingers
washed down with English ale
almost always brings her
from deep in my wishing well.

Too many nights apart
causes my rhymes to infarct.

Roles Without Controls

Rose petals are tarantulas
surrounding our distress
in this seasonal congress
of prey and postulates.

Congruencies are estimates
designed in pentagrams
and contrived in denied dreams
of oasis and ripened dates.

We fulfill both of our roles
without concepts or controls.

Scales

I sit, and sit, and sit,
and wait for the shower
to wash away your choice.

The balance of emotions
between your hidden relief
and my sudden grief
was done unblinded.

The weight will mitigate
when I find a surrogate.

The Second Truth

When I first met you
I knew the second truth.
Who knows the first man
off the moon or the sherpa
guide on Everest?